The Ultimate Guide To
HIP REPLACEMENT RECALL

WARNING: HIP REPLACEMENT RECALL
Metal on Metal Devices

Law Offices of Lisa Douglas
2300 Main
North Little Rock, AR 72114
501-798-0004
739 South 7th Street
Suite 2
Heber Springs, AR 72543
www.HipReplacements.us

DISCLAIMER

This Book is Not Legal Advice

This information is general in nature and should not be relied on as a substitute for legal advice.

This book is provided as an education service by Law Offices of Lisa Douglas.

The purpose of this book is to provide information about metal-on-metal hip replacements. This document is not a source of medical advice and concerned patients should see their orthopaedic surgeon for evaluation.

TABLE OF CONTENTS

FOREWORD

If you can answer YES to any of the following questions, I may be the lawyer for you.

1. Have you received a hip replacement?

2. Are you experiencing pain, swelling, difficulty walking, or hear a clicking noise when you walk?

3. Did you receive your hip replacement between 2003 to 2010?

4. Was your hip implant a metal on metal device?

5. Did you have a metal on metal hip implant and are not currently experiencing symptoms?

If you can answer YES to any of these questions, give us a call at 501-798-0004

WHY THIS BOOK?

I wrote this book because, if you are like most, this is the first time you have been involved in a recall and you have many questions. Many times, I have found the questions come too late and, as a result, the injured victim pays because of his or her lack of information.

By now, you may be receiving letters from the doctor informing you of problems with your implanted device. The first thing that you should never forget is that you should not sign any forms without talking to a lawyer first.

The hip implant company may be asking you to sign a few forms so they can get your records and "handle everything for you." They may have already proposed you settle your claim by offering you money. These types of offers are tempting, but BEWARE. Before you accept this offer, they will require you to sign a release form. This form forever releases them from any further obligation to you. In fact the offer is probably vague, offering compensation for certain out of pocket medical expenses in exchange for signing certain releases. CAUTION: You could be signing away your right to privacy and other legal rights in exchange for little to no compensation.

I encourage you to contact an attorney before agreeing to sign anything. It is possible that your own doctor has been asked to provide you with these documents to sign. **BEWARE:** Do you know what your rights are, do you know what rights you are signing away, do you know what effect this metal on metal implant will have on your health 2, 3, 4 or more years into the future, who will pay for this, will you?

You may have already incurred additional medical expenses because of the faulty metal on metal implant, suffered pain and reduced mobility. You may have already suffered through a revision surgery in an effort to correct the faulty metal on metal implant. You may have suffered loss of income as well.

I wrote this book for **you.** Hopefully you find it will give you some valuable information to consider on your own time BEFORE you hire an attorney and before you sign any forms at the request of your doctor or the hip implant company.

This book is too limited to explore every issue or address each possible question you may have.

Further, this book is not intended to give legal advice and nothing in this book is legal advice. Obtaining this book from me does not create an attorney-client relationship between us. I do not sign up everyone who calls my office that has a hip implant.

Please note that you are not considered a client until we have accepted your case and you have signed a contingency fee contract with us. The information in this book is not medical advice and is not intended to be medical advice. It is not a substitute for medical or other professional advice.

Recalled Metal on Metal Hip Devices May Cause Metallosis

A great concern facing the public now is the failure of metal-on-metal hip implant devices using systems like the recently recalled DePuy ASR hip implants. One concern is due to the tissue damage caused by metallosis that can compromise subsequent revision surgery. Another concern is the potentially long term health risks posed by metallosis.

In August 2010, a recall was issued by DePuy Orthopaedics, a division of Johnson & Johnson, for the company's ASR (Articular Surface Replacement) Hip Resurfacing System and ASR XL Acetabular System total hip replacement, following reports of a higher-than-normal failure rate.

Metallosis

Metallosis occurs when friction from the metal-on-metal hip implant causes the release of potentially dangerous levels of chromium and cobalt ions into the body. According to research, a serum cobalt level of > 7 mg/L is indicative of possible metallosis. A normal serum cobalt level is .19 mg/L.

Metallosis can cause damage to vital organs.

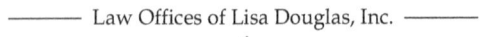

Consequences of metallosis are: ringing in the ears, dizziness, blindness, deafness, nerve damage, headaches, convulsions, hypothyroidism, damage to the heart, brain and/or other vital organs.

Many of the patients who received the DePuy ASR (Articular Surface Replacement) Hip Resurfacing System and ASR XL Acetabular System total hip replacement have filed lawsuits against the company, stating that DePuy did not do enough to warn consumers about the serious side effects associated with these hip implant devices.

But to be fair, there are other hip replacement implant systems out there that are metal on metal devices. It is this metal on metal device that could pose serious long term health problems.

Basic Anatomy of the Hip Joint
and
Implant System

The Hip Joint

The hip joint is a ball-and-socket joint in which a spherical knob or knob like part of one bone fits into a cavity or socket of another.

The ball portion of the hip joint (femoral head) fits into the socket (acetabulum) of the hip bone (pelvis). A properly functioning hip joint is critical for normal everyday activities such as walking, running and climbing.

Hip Implant Systems

During total hip replacement surgery, damaged portions of the hip are removed. The ball (femoral head) is removed and replaced with an artificial ball made of metal or ceramic, and the socket (acetabulum) is removed and replaced with an artificial cup. The cup consists of one or two components made of metal, ceramic or plastic. A stem is also placed inside the femur bone (thigh bone) to support the ball (femoral head).

Currently, in the United States, there are four

different devices to choose from for a total hip replacement. These are:

Metal-on-Polyethylene: The ball is made of metal and the socket is made of plastic (polyethylene) or has a plastic lining.

Ceramic-on-Polyethylene: The ball is made of ceramic and the socket is made of plastic (polyethylene) or has a plastic lining.

Metal-on-Metal: The ball and socket are both made of metal.

Ceramic-on-Ceramic: The ball is made of ceramic and the socket has a ceramic lining.[1]

Resurfacing

During total hip resurfacing surgery, the femoral head is not removed. Instead the femoral head is trimmed and capped with a covering. Any damaged bone and cartilage within the socket are removed and replaced with a shell.[2]

There are certain risks associated with surgery, including hip replacement surgery. The risks of surgery include:
A reaction to the anesthesia

---

[1]http://www.fda.gov/MedicalDevices/ProductsandMedicalProcedures/ImplantsandProsthetics/MetalonMetalHipImplants/ucm241593.htm

[2]Id

Heart attack
Wound infection
Excessive bleeding
Blood clots

After surgery, adverse events may include:
Hip dislocation, when the ball of the thighbone
(femur) slips out of its socket in the hip bone
(pelvis)
Bone fracture
Joint infection
Local nerve damage with numbness/weakness
Device loosening or breakage
Difference in leg lengths
Bone loss (osteolysis)
Depending on the severity of the adverse event(s),
additional surgery may be necessary.[3]

---

[3]http://www.fda.gov/MedicalDevices/ProductsandMedicalProcedu
res/ImplantsandProsthetics/MetalonMetalHipImplants/ucm241594.htm

Metal-on-Metal Hip Implant Systems

Metal-on-Metal (MoM) hip implants consist of a ball, stem and shell, all made of metal materials.

There are two types of MoM hip systems:
Traditional total hip replacement implant
Total resurfacing hip implant[4]

Traditional Metal-on-Metal Total Hip Replacement Implant

Metal-on-Metal total hip replacement systems consist of a metal ball (femoral head), a metal femoral stem inserted into the thighbone, and a metal cup in the hip bone (acetabular component).[5]

Metal-on-Metal hip resurfacing systems consist of a trimmed femoral head capped with a metal covering. Any damaged bone and cartilage within the socket are removed and replaced with a metal cup in the hip bone (acetabular component).

The FDA has approved three metal-on-metal hip resurfacing systems through the premarket

---

[4] http://www.fda.gov/MedicalDevices/ProductsandMedicalProcedures/ImplantsandProsthetics/MetalonMetalHipImplants/ucm241601.htm

[5] Id

approval (PMA) program. They are:

Birmingham Hip Resurfacing (BHR) System,
CONSERVE® Plus Total Resurfacing Hip System, and
Cormet Hip Resurfacing System[6]

---

[6] Id

Concerns about Metal-on-Metal Hip Implant Systems

All artificial hip replacement systems have risks related to implant or material wear. Metal-on-metal hip (MoM) replacement systems have unique risks in addition to the general risks of all hip implant systems.
Because the metal ball and the metal cup slide against each other during walking or running, this friction causes tiny metal particles to wear off of the implant and enter into the tissue space of the hip joint. These metal particles eventually enter the bloodstream.[7] Because of the friction, there is no way to fully avoid the release of these metal particles.

Over time, the metal particles can cause damage to bone and/or tissue of the hip joint.   This may cause the implant to become loose or cause pain.

In addition the metal particles circulating in the bloodstream may cause other types of symptoms or illnesses elsewhere in the body, including effects on the heart, nervous system, and thyroid gland.[8]

---

[7] http://www.fda.gov/MedicalDevices/ProductsandMedicalProcedures/ImplantsandProsthetics/MetalonMetalHipImplants/ucm241604.htm

[8] Id

Patients who have MoM hip implants should be aware of symptoms which indicate hip implant failure.

Common symptoms may include:
Pain in the groin, hip or leg
Swelling at or near the hip joint
A limp or change in walking ability

If these symptoms exist, you should receive a thorough medical examination by your medical doctor to determine the actual cause. Besides a physical exam of the hip, other diagnostic tests to consider in evaluating these symptoms include:
Special imaging tests
Using a needle to remove fluid from around the joint (joint aspiration)
Blood tests, including checking levels of metal ions in the blood
Patients who receive a MoM hip implant should also pay close attention to changes in their general health or new symptoms outside their hip including symptoms related to their:
Heart (chest pain, shortness of breath)
Nerves (numbness, weakness, change in vision or hearing)
Thyroid (fatigue, feeling cold, weight gain)
Kidney (change in urination habits)[9]

---

[9] Id

If you have a MoM hip implant and develop any of the symptoms above, it is very important for you to make an appointment with your medical doctor immediately for further evaluation.

If you have a MoM hip implant and develop any new or worsening symptoms beyond just your hip joint, or if you are referred to a doctors to evaluate new conditions, signs or symptoms, you should let the doctor know that you have a MoM hip implant.[10]

---

[10] Id

General Considerations BEFORE Metal-on-Metal Hip Implantation Surgery

You should not receive a MOM hip replacement implant if:
You have moderate to severe renal insufficiency
You have metal sensitivity (e.g. cobalt, chromium, nickel)
You have a suppressed immune system
You are currently receiving high doses of corticosteroids, or
You are a female of childbearing age[11]

Risks Associated with Metal on Metal hip implants, include but are not limited to the following:

Elevated metal ion levels in the joint and blood.
Development of local inflammatory reactions and lesions including soft tissue masses and tissue necrosis.
Development of potential systemic events related to elevated metal ion levels.[12] (cancer, dementia, nerve damage, and heart damage) .

---

[11] http://www.fda.gov/MedicalDevices/ProductsandMedicalProced ures/ImplantsandProsthetics/MetalonMetalHipImplants/ucm241667.htm

[12] Id

Follow-Up for Metal-on-Metal Hip Patients Developing Local Signs/Symptoms

Clinical and Imaging Evaluation

If you are experiencing local symptoms such as pain or decrease in joint function that appear more than three months after metal-on-metal (MoM) hip implant surgery, a thorough evaluation should be completed by your medical doctor. Assessment should include evaluation for joint infection, implant loosening, fracture and dislocation. Localized lesions that are associated with reactions to the metal debris may also present with pain or a variety of other signs/symptoms including but not limited to:

Local nerve palsy
Palpable mass
Local swelling
Joint dislocation or subluxation

Metal Ion Testing

Metal ion (e.g. cobalt and chromium) levels should be assessed. Increases in metal ion levels suggests device wear.[13]

Although there are currently no commercially available standardized tests to assess metal-ion levels, there are a few laboratories in the U.S. that are able to perform these analyses.

Assessment for Systemic Effects

Patients with evidence of excessive device wear or a localized adverse reaction to metal debris (ARMD) should also be assessed for potential systemic effects of exposure to metal ions. A thorough physical examination should be performed with particular focus on cardiovascular, neurological, renal and thyroid signs/symptoms. [14]

Because metal ions are cleared through the kidneys, a patient who has renal insufficiency may be at higher risk for systemic adverse events.

---

[13] Id

[14] Id

FREQUENTLY ASKED QUESTIONS

How do I know if I have a metal-on-metal hip system?

 Patients are usually told about the type of implant they are receiving prior to the surgery. If you are uncertain about which type you have, you should contact the orthopaedic surgeon who performed your procedure, or you can obtain the surgical records from your medical records. These medical records should indicate the type of device you received.

How often should I follow-up with my orthopaedic surgeon?

Your orthopaedic surgeon will determine how frequently you need to follow-up, based on your health care needs. You may have more frequent follow-up visits depending on the type of hip implant, the outcome of the surgery and your recovery, and the results of blood tests or other diagnostic tests.

If you experience new or worsening symptoms or problems with your hip including pain, swelling, numbness and/or a change in ability to walk, you should contact your orthopaedic surgeon immediately.[15]

What should I discuss with my orthopaedic surgeon at each follow-up appointment?

It is important that you discuss any new or worsening symptoms related to your hip, groin or legs; such as pain, swelling, numbness and changes in your ability to walk, since your last visit.
It is also important that you discuss:
Any changes in your overall health.
Whether you are seeing another doctor for a new condition since receiving your metal-on-metal hip implant.

What symptoms might a metal-on-metal hip implant cause?

Symptoms may include hip/groin pain, local swelling, numbness or changes in your ability to walk or any changes in your overall general health.[16]

Are there other medical effects that can occur with my metal-on-metal hip implant system?

---

[15] http://www.fda.gov/MedicalDevices/ProductsandMedicalProced ures/ImplantsandProsthetics/MetalonMetalHipImplants/ucm241766.htm

[16] Id

Metal particles generated from the friction of the metal on metal device can cause a reaction around the joint, leading to deterioration of the tissue around the joint, loosening of the implant and failure of the device,[17] as well as metallosis, dementia, nerve damage, heart damage, even cancer.

What should I do if I am experiencing problems associated with my metal-on-metal hip implant?

1. You should make an appointment to see your surgeon for further evaluation of your implant.
2. If you experience any new symptoms or medical conditions in your body other than at your hip, you should report these to your primary physician, but be sure and remind them that you have a metal on metal hip implant.

---

[17] Id

What should I discuss with my other health care providers?

If you see a medical doctor for any other symptom outside the hip/groin area, including symptoms related to your heart, nervous system, or thyroid gland, it is of utmost importance that you tell that health care provider that you have a metal-on-metal hip implant. This information may affect the types of diagnostic tests that are performed to further evaluate the cause of your symptoms.

What is a recall?

A recall is an action taken to address a problem with a medical device that violates FDA law. Recalls occur when a medical device is defective, when it could be a risk to health, or when it is both defective and a risk to health.

A recall is either a correction or a removal depending on where the action takes place. Correction - Addresses a problem with a medical device in the place where it is used or sold. Removal - Addresses a problem with a medical device by removing it from where it is used or sold.[18]

---

[18] Id

Who recalls medical devices?

In most cases, a company (manufacturer, distributor, or other responsible party) recalls a medical device on its own (voluntarily). When a company learns that it has a product that violates FDA law, it does two things:
Recalls the device (through correction or removal)
Notifies FDA.[19]

---

[19] Id

A Note From the Author

After reading this book, I hope you have more insight about the health risks of a metal on metal hip replacement devices than when you initially requested this book and began your investigation. This book will give you a head start and get you thinking about the things that can affect your claim. My purpose in writing this book was to equip you with general information about metal on metal hip implant devices and provide you with some things you should know to protect your legal rights. After all, knowledge is power.

If you or a loved one suffered complications after having hip replacement surgery, you may be entitled to compensation. You may have a legal claim for your condition! Don't delay, there is a limited time to file your claim.